David Tennant

Molly Mitchell

Here's David

Is David Tennant the coolest man in the country? The coolest man on the planet? Or the coolest man in the galaxy? After three glorious years as Doctor Who the answers have to be 'yes', 'yes' and 'absolutely yes'!

He's the actor with the X factor and best of all, he's one of the good guys. Ask anyone who knows him and they'll say David is the nicest man they've ever met.

Men like being his friend. Girls like being at his side. His family and his co-stars say they love the fact that fame hasn't changed him one bit. Whether you want to be him or be beside him you're in good company.

So what's his secret? How has the telly-mad boy from Bathgate in Scotland hit the big time in such style? How has he made everything from science fiction to Shakespeare seem so cool?

REACH FOR THE STARS

The young David went to Paisley Grammar, which is a famously sporty school and has produced more than its fair share of politicians and company bosses. With school productions few and far between David always knew he would have to look elsewhere to learn the skills he needed for his future. At first his dad helped him out again. David got a part in a play with the local amateur dramatic group at his dad's church. Then, at just 14, David told his parents he needed more. He asked if he could go to the Saturday youth theatre club set up by the award-winning Royal Scottish Academy of Music and Drama. While they were happy to pay for the Saturday classes, David's mum and dad were worried that their son was setting himself up for a fall. They didn't see how someone from a little-known town in the suburbs of Glasgow could ever really make it in the theatre. Shouldn't David have a fall-back career option in mind?

David's parents sat him down to warn him what a risky path he would be treading as an actor. But David was convinced he had the talent and he was determined to make his own luck. 'I always wanted to act and I never once wavered,' he said, years later. There was already a touch of steel in his soul. And he soon found out that there needed to be. He was about to grow up very fast indeed.

DREAM CATCHER

At 16 David decided to leave school and sign up for a full-time course at the Academy. All he had to do was persuade them to let him in! The course he had chosen was aimed at university students so if he got offered a place David would be one of the youngest students the Academy had ever had.

But David sailed through his audition. The selection panel offered him a place but warned him he was in for a tough few years. He was the youngest person on the course and also the least experienced. 'I was very green when I started there,' David remembers. 'I hadn't really done anything in life and I was surrounded by all these people who were much older and had much more professional experience. I remember spending most of the first couple of years just trying to bluff it.' But being in a real life *Fame Academy* made it all worthwhile. 'Instead of doing double maths at school I was doing something I really loved,' David says with a big wide smile.

13

DAVID'S GOT THE X FACTOR

Right from the start it wasn't just David's tutors who noticed how good he was. Talent scouts and casting agents were invited to as many Academy productions as possible. In 1988 one scout spotted 17-year-old David acting in a ghost story. He called him in for his first professional audition which led to him being cast in ITV's kids show *Dramarama*. It was undoubtedly the biggest moment of his life.

Edging ahead of his older classmates could have hit David's friendships, but he never bragged about his television debut. Making friends – and keeping them – became the hallmark of David's life in and after the Academy.

IT'S ALL IN A NAME ...

David had one final thing to do before leaving theatre school. He had to change his name! On 18 April 1971 he had been born David John McDonald. But in the late 1980s you still needed an Equity card to get paid as an actor and you couldn't sign up for Equity if you had the same name as an existing member. When he returned his form David was told two things. First, there was already another David McDonald on Equity's books. Second, the man was actually acting just across town at the Glasgow Citizen's Theatre! 'It was the first time I saw my name in lights,' David joked with friends after he headed over to take a look. Then he got down to the serious business of re-inventing himself. He needed a new name fast. What would it be?

'How can I describe myself? I'm a skinny streak of nothing. I'm tall, skinny and Scottish.'

After trying everything he could think of he grabbed a copy of a magazine to try and re-ignite his imagination. His eye hit a story about Kirk Brandon, star of the long-forgotten punk band Spear of Destiny. 'I like that,' David thought. So could plain old David McDonald transform himself into the tough-sounding David Brandon? Or should David change his first name instead? He flicked through the magazine a second time. This time his eye fell upon an article about a band called the Pet Shop Boys. Neil Tennant was the super-cool lead singer, Chris Lowe the enigmatic keyboard player. David was a big fan of them both. 'Chris McDonald or David Tennant?' David tried to imagine both names in lights or on screen before choosing the latter. Years later he said he picked it because he thought it sounded slightly more exotic. But in truth there was another reason. He did it to please his mum. Back in Bathgate, Helen hated the fact that her son had to give up his name to succeed. If he had to change it she asked if he could at least stay a David. He agreed straight away and wrote the words 'David Tennant' in block capitals on his Equity form. When the application went through he was ready for his new life to begin. Then all he needed to do was get a job!

It wasn't just *Doctor Who* and *Blake's 7* that obsessed David as a little boy. He was just as gripped by stories about the Loch Ness monster, Big Foot and Yetis.

THE LOW ROAD TO STARDOM

David hit the auditions circuit with his fingers firmly crossed. He was convinced that the perfect job was out there just waiting for him. In a way he was right. He got work within a few weeks of leaving the Royal Academy in Glasgow, but it wasn't exactly an easy ride.

The good news was that he would be acting on stage almost every night for the rest of the summer. The bad news was that the play almost always took place in a different venue. The company was off on a tour of tiny theatres and community halls across the Scottish Highlands and Islands. It was theatre at its most basic and least glamorous. But it was exactly what 20-year-old David needed. When the play finished its run David was back on the auditions circuit. Bearing in mind how young and inexperienced he was, colleagues remember being really impressed that David got another role straight away. But the youngster was about to find out that it was far too early to relax. He was about to get a brutally bad review.

DOWNS AND UPS

The play was called *Merlin* and David remembers it well. 'It was only my second job and the review in *The Scotsman* said: "The cast of 18 are uniformly excellent, with the exception of David Tennant, who lacks any charm or ability whatsoever."' The grown-up David has got the confidence to laugh about that review now. But at the time he was devastated. He was terrified that when that night's crowd came in they would be watching out for him! It would have been incredibly easy to have given it all up and headed back home to start a whole new career. But David didn't. He knew the show had to go on. He knew that to do otherwise would have been to let his colleagues down – and to let himself and his family down as well. 'Just prove them wrong,'

he muttered to himself in the wings as he tried to peer out to see the crowd. Then he turned in a faultless performance. He never got such a bad review again and he had proved just how tough he could be.

BACK ON THE ROAD

When the play ended David went back on the road. He wasn't earning a huge amount of money but he was making plenty of friends and learning about his craft. Like most actors he loved talking shop. Older actors inspired him the most. He lapped up

David's Favourite Music: The Proclaimers, plus The Kaiser Chiefs and – of course – Kylie!

On the Box

Taking curtain calls on stage was a real thrill for David but his heart belonged to TV. The little boy who had sat glued to his favourite science fiction shows was still desperate to act on the small screen and he was determined to become a part of that world for good.

The problem was that in the early 1990s very few major TV shows were made in Scotland. So David was delighted when he won a role in the hit series *Rab C. Nesbitt* in the summer of 1993. And what a role it turned out to be. Every morning David was in the make-up trailer for more than an hour having thick white powder put on his face, bright scarlet lipstick on his lips and a big curly wig on his head! David's character, a barmaid called Davina, was the star of the episode, so David couldn't have cared less if people said such an extreme role might rule him out of other jobs in the future. He thought it was the perfect showcase for his talents, and when his episode was broadcast David was on cloud nine.

ACTING CRAZY

David's next big break was with a BBC comedy called *Takin' Over The Asylum*. It was a tough part to cast. 'They need someone who can believably act 19 and bonkers,' David was told. 'That could be me!' he said. David turned up with his long, dark hair swept back and looking like a typical skinny, scruffy student in a baggy purple sweater and jeans. But when he started to speak he was mesmerising. The director and the rest of the team were blown away by David's audition. He won the role and was signed up for the full series.

When filming began it wasn't just the writers and directors who spotted star quality in David. So did his co-stars. The actress and writer Arabella Weir headed north for her part in the show and met David on the first day of the shoot. 'Blimey, he's brilliant,' was her first impression. 'He was 22 and had only just started acting, yet his confidence and determination were extraordinary.' On a personal level David and Arabella also hit it off straight away. She was nearly ten years older than him but they found they never ran out of things to talk about. They went out for a cheap pizza that first evening in Glasgow and have been best friends ever since.

LONDON CALLING

Everything changed for David when the shoot ended. Arabella headed back south and David asked if he could go with her.

For David the move to London was a huge gamble. He admits he cried with nerves throughout almost all of the six-hour drive down! His big fear was of getting lost on the auditions circuit. It nearly happened. The moment he arrived he was blown away by the sheer talent on display in the capital. He realised he would have to raise his game to compete. So that's exactly what he did. He got a new agent and had some new photographs taken. The black and white photos emphasised his super-sharp cheekbones and sultry eyes. Before long the gamble began to pay off. David landed roles on TV and in the theatre, appearing in *The Bill* and at the National Theatre. Little did he know that just around the corner was an opportunity that would see him transported right across the world!

A HOLLYWOOD STAR?

Can life get much better when you're a young, free, single and successful actor in London? Yes it can. David was off to Hollywood. The casting directors of his first big film thought he was the coolest character they had ever seen. He had the perfect mix of innocence and laid-back cool. So he was the perfect choice to play the hero in *LA Without a Map*.

As the star of the film he was given an air conditioned Winnebago on the edge of the set as well as a mini army of assistants ready to do anything he asked. There was even one man whose sole purpose in life seemed to be to carry a chair around in case David needed to sit down! David remembers that the man was devastated when he said he was perfectly capable of finding his own place to sit. 'He was like: "I've gotta do this, this is my job, if I don't follow you with this chair I'm out of

'I told my mum that I wanted to be the people on the television.'

21

LA. Too well.'

Away from the set David took full advantage of his moment in the sun but in truth he never really intended to stay in America. He joked that his pale Scottish skin couldn't cope with all the sunshine! But really he couldn't cope with all the waiting around. In Hollywood he found that most of his actors were always waiting for a really big job to come along. But David had become an actor because he wanted to work. He was a grafter. He wanted to challenge himself, to take on new roles. Earning a fat pay packet for one job a year wouldn't make him happy. So he headed back to London and threw himself back onto the auditions circuit.

> 'He's very organised. When we lived together I was always teasing him about his alphabetised CDs.' Arabella Weir

TAKING OVER THE TV

For the next few years it was hard to miss David's sharp cheekbones and cheeky grins. He worked here and he worked there before winning a challenging role in *Blackpool*, the genre-busting BBC One series that swerved from reality to fantasy in the blink of an eye. There were dream sequences, dance numbers – and a whole lot of music. Then after *Blackpool*, David entered another world of fantasy – the wild and wonderful world of *Casanova*. He was cast as the legendary Italian lover, the man who is said to have wooed and won more women than most people have had hot dinners! The red-hot writer Russell T Davies had been commissioned to write a red-hot script for the BBC. He delivered. He put together an extraordinary romp of a series. It had pace, it had passion. All it needed was the leading man to bring it all to life.

David was one of the first actors to be shown the script but he just didn't see himself in the role. 'My first reaction was that I wasn't good looking enough,' he said, modestly. But he went for a casting session anyway. That was when he set the screen alight. 'The minute his audition tape started I just went: "That's it." He walked it,' says Russell, who signed David up straight away.

EVEN HEROES HAVE HEROES!

His first big thrill was getting the chance to meet one of his all time heroes, the actor Peter O'Toole. David isn't ashamed to admit that he was hugely star-struck when the pair first met. He even got a photo taken of the pair of them together. Then he pinned it to his fridge door at home so he could keep the connection alive long after the show had been filmed. Little did David know, however, that he would soon be stepping into the role of a lifetime and one which would mean that photos of him would soon be plastered to fridge doors – and bedroom walls – around the country!

Dreaming of the Doctor

Just how did David make his childhood dream come true and win the job as Doctor Who? The simple answer is by working hard and never giving up. For most of his career he had been forced to put his ambition on hold.

The show had been cancelled by the BBC back in 1989 when David was still a student at the Royal Scottish Academy in Glasgow. The last Doctor, Sylvester McCoy, had made his final appearance on 6 December that year, a bad Christmas for David and all the other diehard fans. The BBC said viewers were no longer prepared to put up with wobbly sets or unconvincing villains. So after 26 years the show seemed doomed. But David still kept his hopes alive.

When the internet took hold he started to log on to sci-fi fan sites to read the latest rumours about a possible revival, and like every other fan he had his hopes raised, then dashed, at regular intervals. But after sitting down to watch the one-off television movie the BBC made in 1996 he felt the final nail had been hammered into the programme's coffin. It wasn't that the movie was bad but like everyone else he read that the show had flopped in the US. That meant no more American money for a long term revival. No more *Doctor Who*! But David is a fighter. He began to think laterally. If he couldn't go on screen as the Doctor, couldn't he win a role in the show elsewhere? He decided that if he ever saw an audition for a new theatrical version of the show – even a pantomime – then he would cancel anything to be there. Whatever it took David would get to play the Doctor.

THE RETURN OF THE DOCTOR

In the late summer of 2003 the news was full of the story that *Doctor Who* was coming to TV with a vengeance. There was a top new writer – the still red-hot Russell T Davies who had written sensational scripts for *Queer As Folk* and, of course, would also write *Casanova*. And, frustratingly for David, there was a top new Doctor – the tall and icy Christopher Eccleston.

The new prime time series was to start filming in 2004 and would be broadcast in the late spring of 2005. David's childhood dreams looked to be in tatters. He was convinced that if Christopher's Doctor was a flop then the show would never be revived again. He was also convinced that if he was a hit then Christopher wouldn't jump ship for many, many years.

ALL ABOARD

When the first episode was broadcast it was clear that the show would be a sensation. Christopher's new Doctor, officially deemed the ninth, won rave reviews. The revived show was an immediate hit. More than 10 million people watched *Rose*, the first episode that had cleverly re-introduced the Doctor to old and new viewers alike. The show even beat Saturday night favourites Ant and Dec who had brought David Beckham on to their show to try and see off the sci-fi competition.

Long-standing fans were amazed at the quality of the new production. Gone were those dodgy sets and dodgier villains. In had come CGI special effects and Hollywood style backdrops. There were amazing all-star casts. Best of all were the scripts. They were funny and intelligent. If David thought the show he had watched as a boy had been good then this was brilliant. From killer wheelie bins to the return of the Autons, the Slitheens and, of course, the Daleks (which could now fly as well as making it up stairs) it was clearly a series to remember. 'I watched it all and marvelled at it and I thought it was brilliant and that Chris was just fantastic,' says the very generous David.

Critics and viewers all agreed that Christopher and Billie Piper (Rose) were perfectly cast in their new roles. 'If you're an alien, how come you sound like you're from the north?' was Billie's favourite line in that first episode. Christopher's deadpan reply that lots of planets have a north was pitch perfect. Within weeks it seemed the pair were well on their way to becoming national institutions. If they wanted jobs for life then they had them. David was one of the very few people to know it was all about to change.

A DREAM COMES TRUE

It was the middle of April 2005 and David was enjoying a few days in Scotland with his mum and dad. The family were in the kitchen having breakfast when Sandy turned on the TV so they could watch the news. David was on it.

The BBC had finally confirmed one of the biggest stories in broadcasting – that David was going to replace Christopher Eccleston and become the tenth actor to play Doctor Who. His phone started to ring, and hardly stopped for weeks. 'Have you got something you want to tell us?' mum and dad asked their son with a smile as the news broadcast ended. And he was thrilled finally to be able to tell them the full story.

'The whole process was a high voltage secret and I hadn't been able to tell anyone, not even my parents,' he says now. He'd been

Favourite Doctor Who:
A tie between Peter Davison and Tom Baker.

28

approached months earlier, when Christopher had first voiced his fears of being typecast in the new part and ground down by its punishing production schedule. 'What did you say when they offered it to you?' his parents asked him in Glasgow. They knew just how much this job meant to their sci-fi mad son. 'I didn't say anything,' David told them. He hadn't. He remembers that all he could do that day was laugh, because it had all seemed so surreal.

THE 10TH DOCTOR

Amazingly enough, he didn't even say yes the moment the laughter stopped. He felt he needed time to think about it and admits he had 'a few wobbles' about what he might be taking on. But after two days of worrying, David made his decision. 'I just woke up one morning and thought, what on earth are you thinking of, just do it. You're only the 10th bloke who's ever got to play this part and you'd be kicking yourself for the rest of your life if you missed it. I decided I wasn't going to be the guy who watched someone else play it. So I said yes.'

Everyone was ecstatic. There had been plenty of rumours that other famous names were up for the role. But Russell T Davies said David was 'absolutely the only name in the frame to take over' from Christopher. He'd adored his performances on *Casanova*. He knew David could interpret and deliver his words better than anyone. Losing Christopher after just one season was a blow to the series. But with David on board everyone was sure they could overcome it. Everyone was right.

A DATE WITH DESTINY

Billie was pretty much the first person David met when he turned up for work on his first day on set. 'She was welcoming, wonderful and easy to work with,' he said with a huge sigh of relief. And he had been surprisingly nervous. 'The worst bit of being the new boy on set was all the hoo-ha that comes with the show – the fact that everyone is so fascinated by it. That makes it the most wonderful job in the world but also the most terrifying. When I finished my first day of filming I remember going home and collapsing. Everything had been building up and it was exhausting.'

The following night David couldn't just go back to his hotel and crash. The production team were throwing a big welcome dinner for their new cast member. The other special guest was the actor and writer Stephen Fry who was about to play one of the next set of celebrity cameo roles in the series. David sat next to Billie and her then boyfriend Amadu and started to bond with them both. By the time the party broke up just before midnight he knew he was well on the way to making some lifelong friends.

NOTES FROM OLD DOCTORS

The real work began the following day. The team had a 13-episode series and a Christmas special to make. Sitting in his dressing room David looked at the good luck cards he had been sent by Tom Baker and Peter Davison and smiled. He would make them proud. This was the role he had been born to play. He would be the coolest, sharpest, funniest and most believable Doctor yet.

> 'Screen kisses? I love them. Especially with David.' Billie Piper

MEET THE NEW DOCTOR WHO …

Stepping out on to the set, the first part of the transformation was already clear to see. David's new clothes marked him out as a very modern man. He likes to call it 'geek chic'. The increasingly big, spiky hair. The pinstriped suits and the plimsolls. He jokes that the overall look was modelled on none other than Jamie Oliver. David had watched the chef walk on to *Parkinson* in his signature scruffy/smart garb the previous year. He had called Russell T Davies and suggested dressing his Doctor in something similar. Russell had seen the very same clip and had already asked the BBC's wardrobe people to pull together some suitable outfits. David looked sensational in them. His on screen image was set. Now all he had to do was act.

'Hello. New teeth. Now, where were we?' Those had been David's now famous first words as he regenerated into the tenth Doctor – looking young and fresh faced with his hair all spiked up and wild. But there was so much more than just comedy to his first full appearance in the 2006 Christmas special and in his first series as a whole. The killer Christmas trees and scary Santas in the hour long special never came close to stealing the show. Everyone's attention was on the new Doctor. Everyone wanted to know what he would be like. And that included Rose. She certainly approved. 'Can I just say, travelling with you – I just love it. You're so different!' she said at one point. Billie admits she could hardly have put it better herself. She loved travelling with David too.

'The new fellow, Tennant, is excellent.'
Tom Baker

CELEBRITY SHOWCASE

He's been on screen with his dad twice. In the Doctor Who *episode* The Unicorn and the Wasp *and on* Ready Steady Cook.

When the Christmas special was in the can (most of it had been filmed amidst a lot of fake snow in West London in July) the team moved on to the rest of the series. The first episode David worked on was called *New Earth*. It was set in the 5,000,000th century with the Doctor and Rose heading to a luxury hospital in mankind's new home. Zoe Wanamaker was back as the paper-thin, villainess-in-chief Lady Cassandra. She says she relished her time playing alongside David and Billie (she jokes that her favourite line was when her spirit was transferred into Rose's body. 'Oh my god, I'm a chav,' she moaned).

Zoe was only the very first of a long line of famous co-stars to shake David's hand as the series progressed. He acted alongside Peter Kay, Anthony Head, Maureen Lipman and Pauline Collins to name just a few. 'It's like a who's who of acting talent,' David told pals back in London. He loved it. What he was too modest to say was that very few of these famous name stars could take much attention away from him. Celebrity guests would come and

go. The Doctor would always need to rise above. 'David is at the centre of every scene so he has to have great charisma and invention,' said Russell T Davies, lost in admiration of his new star. 'He can find lightness even in the darkest of scenes. He has brought real intelligence to the role as well as perfect comic timing'. And as the filming of that first series drew to its close Russell says David's magic was as strong as ever. 'I still find myself thinking "I've never seen him do that before". He brings out the best in the whole crew. You never want him to have bad lines of dialogue. You want to do your best for him.'

SUPER COOL

Other insiders agreed that David was the super cool, super talented heart of the show. 'David's fab. He gets the most incredibly long scripts to learn. It's almost a game seeing how many lines they can throw at him but he never falters,' said Gillane Seaborne, series producer of *Doctor Who Confidential* who watched David at work almost every day. David tried to repay every last compliment. He said he had loved Russell's scripts on *Queer As Folk* and *Casanova*, he adored them on *Doctor Who*. 'They are a real gift. I get to be the guy with all the best lines and the wit and it really has to be played at a lick. It's a challenge but you never want to let anyone down. Each script you get is more inventive, funnier, wilder and more extraordinary than the last.'

A KISS FROM A ROSE

On the subject of compliments, David was quick to throw some over to Billie as well. 'She's funky and modern, sexy and sassy. She's a brilliant actress and in every take she's got something new. She makes it all look effortless,' he said. And he loved having a laugh with her. The big story of the first series was their first kiss. David and Billie brought real passion to the relationship between Doctor and Assistant. So were they, weren't they? Would they or wouldn't they? It was a perfect tease for viewers. But on set it was all played for laughs. 'Screen kisses? I love them. Especially with David,' Billie told the press with a big wide smile. She said it had taken them three takes to get their first big kiss right, then added perhaps a little too much information by saying: 'We didn't do tongues because that day we had been eating egg and cress sandwiches for lunch.'

LIVING THE DREAM

Three months had gone by since the spectacular Christmas special. Now, on Saturday 15 April, 2006, the new episodes were ready for transmission. What would everyone think? David's first lesson was that the media coverage was intense. Hundreds of reporters and photographers had headed along the M4 to Cardiff for the show's launch press conference. His face was on almost every magazine cover. He and Billie were looking down from billboards across London. And nearly 9 million people were watching when *New Earth* began.

One week later almost a million more viewers tuned in to see David use his real Scottish accent in the far darker *Tooth and Claw* episode staring Pauline Collins as Queen Victoria – with a very scary were-wolf on her tail. The series was becoming a massive word of mouth hit. Tom Baker, David's ultimate hero, was one of the first to congratulate his young follower. He said he had barely watched the show since leaving it more than 20 years earlier. But he had watched these early episodes and said David was 'excellent' in his role. Hard-to-please sci-fi fans also hit the internet to post positive messages. Everyone from eight-year-old boys to 80-year-old women were coming up to David in the street saying they thought he was fantastic. Everything was looking great and David had just signed up to film a second series of the show later in the year. But there was a problem. He had just been told that Billie wouldn't be at his side.

Favourite Place for a Holiday: Good old Bonnie Scotland.

A doctor needs an assistant

David hated saying goodbye to Billie. After all the 6am starts, 13-hour days and 11-day fortnights they had become incredibly close. 'We're the only two constants in the show so we are in rehearsal on set and in camera together pretty much every day.

It's nice to spend time with other regular characters when they have scenes but sometimes you don't see those guys for ages. Billie's the only person I know I'm going to see every day,' David said. And because they were inseparable on set they pretty much stayed that way on rare days off as well. David got on well with Billie's family and she was a favourite of his.

Her decision to leave *Doctor Who* was no surprise. David totally understood that she wanted more time and more professional freedom. He also knew that they would stay friends for life – as they proved when he was pretty much the only 'celebrity' guest at her 2008 wedding to Laurence Fox.

But what of the Doctor?

All summer the media was alive to rumours of who David would be acting alongside the following season. The feisty *Torchwood* star Eve Myles was said to be an early front runner. Then there was the story that Noel Clarke's Mickey Smith would join the Tardis as the Doctor's first male assistant. But

David knew that Russell and the rest of the production team had their eye on someone else. Russell told David who it was and asked his opinion. David said two words. 'Absolutely. Yes.' So the young, barely known actress Freema Agyeman was called over to Cardiff for a top secret audition.

FREEMA AGYEMAN

It was a bold choice, not least because Freema had played a minor role in the previous series. She had actually been killed off in episode 12. If she came back as David's new side-kick this would have to be glossed over in the script. Her audition would have to be pretty good to make all that extra effort worthwhile. So little wonder she was terrified. Then David did something wonderful. The night before her audition Freema was holed up in a Cardiff hotel and taken out for a meal with one of the production

'David's fab. He gets the most incredibly long scripts to learn. It's almost a game seeing how many lines they can throw at him but he never falters.'
Doctor Who Confidential producer Gillane Seaborne

crew. She came back to her room to find something under her door. It was a handwritten note from David. It almost made her cry. 'It was really encouraging and just told me to relax and go for it. It meant the world to me,' she says. It proved what a kind man David was. It revealed that he would never forget his own roots. He remembered all too well how tough it had been for him to be the new boy, trying to step into Christopher Eccleston's boots what felt like a thousand lifetimes ago. He knew Freema would be feeling the same fear as she tried to step into Billie's shoes. Offering the hand of friendship was the least he could do. Especially as he was determined that she should get the job. 'She was a joy to work with,' he remembered of her cameo role earlier in the year. He wanted more of the same in the future. So he was more pleased than anyone when she turned in a blinding audition. She got the part. Then the rollercoaster ride began in earnest.

'When David's around I find it much easier to work because of his energy. He makes it all happen.'
Freema Agyeman

SASSY MARTHA

Freema was re-invented as the sexy, sassy Martha Jones. 'I'm delighted. She's not only very talented and very beautiful, she's also great fun,' David said. And he knew from the previous season that if you're going to spend so much time with someone you'll have to be able to share a few laughs with them. He and Freema were giggling pretty much from the off. 'They're terrific together,' Russell said after watching them read through their first few scenes.

David particularly liked how grounded his co-star was. She was very aware how big a break she had been given. Just one year earlier she had been struggling to find acting jobs and had been renting out and selling *Doctor Who* videos in Blockbuster Video. Now she was on the show. When she and David talked about how bizarre an actor's life can be they found they had a few other things in common. Just like David she had paid her acting dues in Sun Hill police station by taking a few roles in *The Bill*. On a personal level David loved that Freema was just as fiercely protective of her private life as he was about his. Just like him she hated to talk publicly about relationships. It was clear that they were going to get along just fine.

GETTING STARTED ON THE NEW SERIES

David's second series of the show was to be even more dramatic than his first. Budgets had allegedly been increased to almost £800,000 an episode. It was a vast amount for an in-house BBC show. But it was money well spent. The Doctor and Martha were in World War One. They were in 1930s New York. They found themselves on alien planets and in modern day London. And like before they acted alongside some stellar guest stars. We saw Mark Gatiss, Derek Jacobi, Michelle Collins, Ardal O'Hanlon and the return of John Barrowman's Captain Jack. David and Freema even shared a bed in one episode – a new departure for the Doctor and his Assistant, though nothing was quite as it seemed.

'It's hard work but it feels like playtime as well,' was Freema's verdict. She loved having David on set and at her side. 'When David's around I find it much easier to work because of his energy. He makes it all happen,' she said.

'On set we're surrounded by props and monsters and explosions and things often go wrong. When they do, we say to each other: "Oh well, at least we've got David." We put the camera on him and it just comes to life.' Doctor Who *producer* Russell T Davies

**Favourite Cars:
A Skoda (no,
really!) until he
bought a Toyota
Prius.**

For his part David loved the humour that still broke through even the darkest of episodes. His deadpan delivery and fabulously versatile face brought even the most ordinary lines alive. 'Many things about this are not good,' he would say as some new peril threatened the Tardis. Off the set he and Freema carried on having fun. He wound her up by pretending to be a mad fan when she did a London-based radio phone-in one day. When they had the chance to go out for rare meals in Cardiff fellow diners said they were incredibly relaxed in each other's company.

THE WRITING'S ON THE WALL

But for all the laughs a few cracks had begun to show. David noticed that the working days were getting even longer as he filmed this 13-episode series. The scripts were even more challenging and complex – notably the hugely praised *The Shakespeare Code*, some of which was filmed out of Cardiff and at the genuine Globe Theatre in London. There were more late night shoots and there was less time for any mornings off so everyone could catch their breath. Insiders say David and the *Doctor Who* team faced one of the most punishing schedules in British TV. In Russell T Davies they also had one of the most demanding task-masters in the business. He oversaw every element of every episode. If he wasn't writing a script he was forcing endless revisions to other people's words so the dialogue sparkled. *Doctor Who* was his baby. He was prepared to do whatever it took to keep it on form. So in May 2007 Russell told David that Martha Jones was in for a sticky end. He wasn't sure that the character was going in the right direction, so it had to be axed.

THE END OF MARTHA?

Of course David's Doctor was as safe as houses. Russell was still lost in admiration for how well the actor fitted the role. He had some extraordinary new plots and twists in store for the following series and he knew David could bring them to life better than anyone. As the news of Freema's departure hit the media David's phone started to ring off the hook. Everyone wanted to know who would be at his side in the next series. David wasn't allowed to say. But he was totally thrilled at the choice. He had a feeling the next series was going to be better than ever.

CATHERINE TATE

'I do get called "nice" a lot but I have my dark moments.'

Catherine Tate had exploded into David's on-screen life in the 2006 Christmas special, *The Runaway Bride.* Her mad, mouthy character, Donna Noble had been one of the few women to face up to his Doctor at his own level. She was fearless, even when she was afraid. She was funny almost every second she was on screen. Not every die-hard fan had liked her in that first show. But David thought she was totally brilliant – and he hated that the script said she walked away when he asked her to join him in the Tardis for good.

Having her back as Freema's full-time replacement gave him a whole new lease of life. 'She was my dream casting,' he said. He felt totally comfortable at her side. He liked that he and Catherine were so close in age. He was 35 when they filmed *The Runaway Bride*, she was 38. Running around with her was a total change from running around with his twenty-something assistants.

He liked it. But was Catherine ready for the sheer madness of being in the *Doctor Who* family?

ONE OF THE FAMILY

'It's more than just a job,' David warned his new friend as the news leaked out. 'You'll start going into supermarkets and see your face on cakes.' Or, he might have said, on underwear. Official and unofficial *Doctor Who* related merchandising was everywhere in 2007. The kind of action figures David had collected as a boy in Bathgate were only the start. Now he really did see his face on everything from sheets to sweets and from calendars to car stickers. He also warned Catherine about the workload she would face in the Tardis. The usual round of stellar guest stars and top notch scripts were being lined up. The series would include episodes featuring a young Agatha Christie (and a killer wasp), a life or death decision to make in Pompeii, and a moving recon-ciliation in *The Doctor's Daughter* (which would kick off David's latest off-screen love affair). There were big cliff-hangers and tough two-part episodes to ratchet up the tension even more.

PARTNERS IN CRIME

While filming behind closed doors on the set in Wales David made a few good natured digs about Catherine's comic talents. 'She's been given half of my funny one-liners. They're the ones I would have had before. Now she is here she gets them,' he moaned with a smile. But he already knew Catherine was a particularly generous performer. Their award-winning 2007 *Comic Relief* sketch had proved that. The clip was a classic. David pulled on a brown corduroy jacket and tie and came on stage as a suitably scruffy, unshaven English teacher to Catherine's stroppy school-girl Lauren. 'My name is Mr Logan. I'm your new English teacher, nice to meet you all,' he began.

'Sir, are you English, sir,' Lauren interrupted, true to form.

'No, I'm Scottish.'

It didn't go down very well. 'So is this lesson Double English or Double Scottish?' Lauren asked after yet more questioning. The fun continued until Catherine gave David the big line. 'Are you the Doctor?' Lauren fired out at last.

'Doctor Who?' David got to ask after a perfectly timed pause, winning the biggest laughs of the night.

STAMINA OF A TIME LORD

Back in Wales David's superhuman energy was still managing to impress his colleagues. 'People can get tired and ratty on set but David never does,' said Russell. Just like Freema before her, Catherine said everyone else always picked up on David's good humour. He liked being a team player, he was never too grand to miss out on any crew birthday parties or celebrations. 'He stands his round in the pub,' one said of him. It was perhaps the highest compliment that one colleague can ever pay another. But as an old hand on the show David knew that filming the episodes and having fun on set was only one part of the *Doctor Who* madness. He warned Catherine that the world would go totally mad when the time

AWARD AFTER AWARD

He had won his first Best Actor award for *Doctor Who* back in 2006. Two years on and his trophy cabinet was bulging. Even Ant and Dec were getting a run for their money at most awards shows. And it wasn't just acting awards that came David's way. No-one could come close when it came to the 'most eligible men' and 'sexiest star' awards. Brad Pitt, David Beckham, George Clooney, Orlando Bloom – they all got left in David's wake by loved-up fans. Women said there was a very simple reason for David's on going attraction – he was so clearly comfortable in his own skin. 'He looked better in his mid to late thirties than he did in his twenties because

he's learned how to relax. He's not pretending. He's a nice guy with nothing to prove and that sends off an incredibly attractive vibe,' said beauty writer Eve Black who met him at a 2008 awards ceremony. 'If you think he's tall, dark and handsome on screen – you should see him in the flesh girls!' she added afterwards.

To be honest, most girls had already suspected as much. Even the normally all-male world of *Doctor Who Magazine* was being turned upside down by David's super-fans. 'We've started to get letters from girls. I would never have imagined this happening,' said the magazine's long time editor Clayton Hickman. And this wasn't Clayton's only compliment for David. He was able to tell him that his readers had voted David 'Best Doctor', over perennial favourite Tom Baker.

A WELCOME SHOCK FOR THE FANS

So could anything go wrong for David? After three years in the Tardis it was perhaps inevitable that a few critics might line up and try to drag him down. Amazingly some took pot shots at his appearance. Everyone loved his mad, spiky hair. His sideburns didn't go down so well. One commentator said that they were growing so big and bushy that they were scarier than some of the aliens. Then the *Sunday Mirror*'s show business writer Kevin O'Sullivan took a swing. 'Is *Doctor Who* really any good?' He criticised the 'mad-eyed over-acting from David Tennant'. But it hardly mattered. As his third full series drew to a close interest in David hit an all time high.

10 MILLION TUNE IN

The craziness hit the peak in the final, two-part episode that began with the *The Stolen Earth* in July. It was magical. Billie, Freema, John Barrowman and Elizabeth Sladen were all on board. The Daleks were all around. The cliff-hanger end to the first show had David hit by a Dalek death ray and carried into the Tardis where his body began to repair and – worse – to regenerate. Did this mean that David, like Christopher Eccleston before him, had decided to hand over the role to another actor? James Nesbitt, Stephen Fry, Rhys Ifans and Robert Carlyle were all said to be lined up as possible replacements. The hype was such that a staggering 10 million people tuned in to the regeneration episode. That was almost exactly half the entire TV audience of the night. And these turned out to be very keen fans. More than 2,500 actually called the fake phone number that appeared on screen at one point, just to see who might answer it (it wasn't David).

Wrong numbers or not, to 10 million people's huge relief David was still there when the starburst of light and energy of the partial regeneration had lifted. His time as the Time Lord was far from up. As an actor there was still a huge amount that he wanted to do. David still had a lot of surprises to spring.

Beyond the Tardis

Some actors like to play things safe. They like to find a niche, win long running jobs and pretty much sleepwalk through their careers. Not David. In his mind the only downside to being Doctor Who had been the fear of being typecast.

He fought against it by taking as many other jobs as possible when he had a few weeks off. He had long since built up a name as one of the hardest working men in show business. Now he wanted to prove he was one of the bravest and the best.

It had begun right back in his first year on *Doctor Who*. While he had been having his top secret casting sessions with Russell and the team he had been playing a very different character on stage in Bath and Edinburgh. The role was as Jimmy Porter in the dark, classic play *Look Back in Anger*. It had always been a controversial play and Jimmy was one of the least attractive characters in modern drama. Many actors wouldn't want to play it in case it ruled them out of softer roles in the future. But David loved the challenge of taking it on. His Jimmy Porter was viciously unpleasant. 'David Tennant spits out his nastiest lines like mouthwash,' wrote one critic. His portrayal conjured up the ultimate angry young man. When David played the part at the Royal Lyceum Theatre in Edinburgh his reviews were sensational. He won the Critics Award for Best Male Performance in Scottish Theatre. It was a huge professional honour.

TAKING A WALK ON THE WILD SIDE

Playing a bad guy on the stage was one thing. But it wasn't enough for David. He wanted to take a walk on the wild side on television and then on the big screen as well. He accomplished the TV goal with his portrayal of Brendan Block in ITV's *Secret Smile* in 2005. David was creepy in the extreme. He was totally believable as a very modern, very nasty and very unbalanced man. Then David helped take the world's cinemas by storm.

He was cast as the fabulously deranged Barty Crouch Jr in *Harry Potter and the Goblet of Fire*. In the scheme of things it was a small role. But David loved being involved in 'a huge great monster of a film'. He was well aware that everyone who is anyone in British acting had been in at least one of the Harry Potter movies. He was thrilled to add his name to the list. And he was thrilled that his 'good doctor' persona had been left far behind. He adored playing one of poor Harry's death-eater enemies. When *Doctor's Who*'s Russell T Davies saw David's performance in the film he described it as 'a perfect little distillation of evil'. Russell was thrilled that David had jumped so far out of his BBC comfort zone on the big screen. But there was one small link to David's old role. Barty Crouch had a bit of a *Doctor Who*-style regeneration moment when David's face appeared amidst the special effects at a key point in the adventure.

HARRY POTTER

When the film finally had its world premiere, in London's Leicester Square in November 2005, David made a rare trip up the red carpet to face the paparazzi. It was the biggest film premiere of the year. David looked totally comfortable and effortlessly cool wearing a white T-shirt with Audrey Hepburn's picture on underneath his black dinner jacket (the effortlessly elegant Hepburn is his all-time favourite female film star). Some said David got more attention from the crowds than even Madonna and Lourdes, who headed up the red carpet just after him.

Having played such an evil character on screen he proved he was still a good bloke in real life. When reporters asked him about the atmosphere on set he was unstinting in his praise of Daniel Radcliffe, Emma Watson and Rupert Grint. 'They're great, just fabulous. I think that if I was their age and I was the most famous teenager in the world I'd just be messed up. But they're so not. They really have their heads screwed on. I admire them all enormously,' he shouted to the press at the after premiere party.

Over the next few days David sat back and watched while the film worked its magic. It was an immediate hit in the UK and took just three days to make $100 million at the US box office. It then went on to become, for a while, the fastest selling DVD of all time. It was all just a little bit different to *LA Without a Map* and gave David a great calling card for Hollywood, if he ever decided to explore that option again.

IN POLE POSITION

Having scrabbled for every audition going at the start of his career David was able to pick and choose his jobs now he had hit his prime. The only thing that would have stopped him was a lack of time or energy. He vowed to make the former – he was a Time Lord, after all. And Dynamo-David never lacked extra reserves of energy. Old friends who found themselves needing a bit more down time as their thirties got under way were constantly amazed that David's action-man tendencies were as strong as ever. He did sometimes get a few heavy colds. But he reckons he'd never had full-blown flu until 2005 when it struck him as he began filming *The Quatermass Experiment* for BBC4. Even then he was back on his feet within a couple of days.

'Matt Smith's got an extraordinary journey coming up in all sorts of ways … I could tell he was very up for it, though, and excited in all the right ways.'

David reckons part of his 'always on' energy comes from within. But part comes from the constant challenges he sets himself. 'Why play one part when you can play two?' he asked himself. Or maybe even three.

Favourite Stars: Audrey Hepburn and John Cleese.

ON THE STAGE

That was the task he set himself when he first triumphed at the Royal Shakespeare Company. In his first season at Stratford upon Avon David hit the stage in three plays, *The Comedy of Errors*, *The Rivals* and *Romeo and Juliet*. It was almost unprecedented, not least because David played one of the leads in each play. It meant he faced a manic series of overlapping rehearsals. Then he had to take to the stage for more than 200 sold-out performances. Being with the RSC made David feel fantastic. It was the gold standard of acting, the place where all his professional heroes had shone. Once you've been in that company you know you will never lose the respect of your peers. The only problem David had that first season was getting to know his fellow actors. With so many roles to play, and so few afternoons or evenings off, he felt he missed out on some of the social side of the job. He couldn't join in much of the fun in the actors' favourite pub, the Dirty Duck, by the river just up from the main stages in Stratford. But he did leave Stratford with many happy memories. He was already hoping that one day he might do it all again.

TREADING THE BOARDS

'Until recently the National Theatre and the Royal Shakespeare Company seemed a million miles away. Then, suddenly, Dame Judi Dench is across the corridor!'

Fast forward to the summer of 2008 and David went back to Stratford in triumph. His modern-day *Hamlet* was set to become a total theatrical sensation. It was the year television's coolest man made Shakespeare the hottest ticket in town. The madness started early. When the Royal Shakespeare Company confirmed that David would be in the play its phones started to ring off the hook. In Stratford the entire four-month run sold out within six hours. Every single ticket for the London production sold even faster. Still his fans didn't give up. Tickets changed hands on places like eBay for up to £1,000 a pair. Every day queues of people lined up outside the box offices desperate to buy 'returns'. From the first night of rehearsals even bigger queues formed for autographs and photographs at the stage door.

With so much fuss going on it was easy to forget what a gamble David was taking by appearing live on stage at all. 'It's not like television or film where re-takes and good editing can make even a bad performance look good,' says fellow actor Martin Evans. 'On stage you only have one chance to get it right. You're totally exposed, night after night. If audiences don't like you then you feel it. If people walk out half-way though a performance you can sometimes see them. It can be devastating for your confidence and that's why so many big stars don't ever go back to their theatrical roots. They're just too worried about it all going wrong.'

David admitted that his colleague was right about the pressure. 'All plays are tough,' he said. 'It's ghastly. Every time I do a play I have a moment when I think I'll never do one again. You're on stage and you're composing the speech you're about to give: "Ladies and Gentlemen, terribly sorry, but I have to leave the stage now and throw up in my dressing room". It's a fear that never goes away. And it's even tougher with Shakespeare. You feel the weight of all those ghosts, all those wonderful performances and you know you have to be good just to compete.' A further complication for David was that this production was always going to be controversial. It was played in modern dress and the set was a *Big Brother* style mass of mirrors. Traditionalists might hate it. If they did, they could punish the cast by reacting badly to the whole thing.

Favourite Films: *Breakfast At Tiffany's, Twelve Angry Men*, all of the early *Star Wars* films as well as *Marnie, The Birds, Psycho* and almost anything else by Alfred Hitchcock.

CURTAINS UP!

So by the time opening night arrived even David was struggling to maintain his legendary cool. Inside the theatre critics from all over the country were sitting ready to give their verdicts. Outside, television cameras were filming the crowds and waiting for the audience's reactions. If David put a single foot wrong the whole world would know about it straight away. The tension was almost impossible to bear. Could David pull it off?

HAMLET

The thunderous applause at the end of the play told him that he had succeeded. His fellow actors, including *Star Trek*'s Patrick Stewart who played Claudius and Mariah Gale as Ophelia, got loud cheers as they took their curtain calls. But David triggered the standing ovation that never seemed to end. People in the first few rows of the theatre said there were tears in his eyes as he finally left the stage, gripping his co-stars' arms and shaking with excitement. For the rest of the night David was the talk of Stratford – and beyond. The pubs and bars were full of people saying how his performance had blown them away. Anyone who had thought he was simply a famous face from TV were eating their words. He was the real deal. And the following day all the newspapers confirmed it.

The play's director, Gregory Doran, was ecstatic that the gamble of employing someone better known for fighting aliens had paid off. He had never doubted David's talents, or his ability to draw an audience. But he had feared that patronising theatre critics might have attacked him out of spite. He was thrilled that David's acting had blown such fears out of the water. And he joked that David's pulling power kept on growing. Absolutely everyone wanted to see him on stage. 'People I haven't spoken to for years phone me up saying: "My daughter would really like it if you could help us get some tickets." And I have to say that tickets are just impossible to get.'

WHERE FOR ART THOU DAVID?

The fact that children who would normally run a mile from a Shakespeare play were badgering their parents to get tickets for David's performance in *Hamlet* wasn't lost on other theatre insiders. David Lister of the *Independent* newspaper put it best: 'There was an unusual sight in the audience: teenagers and even younger children watching the three-and-a-half hour play with rapt attention. These children and teenagers, fans of Tennant as Doctor Who on TV, had clearly made the running, asking their parents to take them or buying tickets for themselves. And they loved what they saw.'

The madness continued when David and the cast headed south to London. They were performing for a month at the Novello Theatre in Covent Garden. People camped on the streets overnight when tickets were first released to the public. By the time the Box Office opened at 10am there were nearly 300 people in the queue. No surprise that every seat for the four-week run was sold by the end of just one day. No surprise either that when the show did open in its new home the reviews were just as good. David hadn't lost any of his magic by moving south from Stratford. Some said he had actually gained even more confidence and control. 'The man from TV is an actor to be reckoned with,' wrote one online critic. 'He's more talented than anyone ever realised.'

Least Favourite Things: Moths and Astrology!

ANOTHER DIMENSION

Ask any of David's colleagues what they like most about him and you'll get a mix of different replies. Some, like Freema Agyeman, say they like his energy and his ability to lift the whole set on a low day. Some, like Russell T Davies, say they like his willingness to take on whatever challenge the writers can throw at him. Some, like Arabella Weir, like his loyalty, kindness and honesty. Others, like Royal Shakespeare Director Michael Boyd, say they like his open spirit and his ability to connect with audiences of all ages.

But everyone agrees on something. They all say that David has got the most wicked sense of humour around. He loves dirty jokes, has a real school-boy laugh and is famous on sets as a compulsive practical joker. He likes taking the mickey out of everyone. Better still, he never minds if they fight back and have a laugh at his expense as well.

Favourite Charities: Headway: the brain injury association, the Association for International Cancer Research, the Accord Hospice, Paisley in Glasgow.

THE FUTURE IS BRIGHT

David is a man who slogged his guts out to make his childhood dream come true. He turned his life around without treading on anyone else's toes or pulling anyone else down. The smiling face that adorns so many bedroom walls and looks out from so many magazine covers is the same face that his friends and family see in private. This most talented of actors certainly isn't acting when he plays Mr Nice Guy. That's the real David Tennant. That's the man who has never changed – even though the world around him has gone crazy. It's worth noting that his best friends are his old friends. They're the ones who know they can call him for advice at midnight, however hard he is working or however tired he's become. They're the ones who

say his silly jokes and offbeat humour will pick them up on the lowest of days. They're the ones who say the David we see today is almost exactly the same as the one they've always known. A bit better looking, perhaps. A bit better groomed, sometimes, and a whole lot braver in the kind of wild clothes he will wear. But one thing never changes. He's always the same great actor, the same good friend and the same ice cool good guy.

First published in hardback in Great Britain in 2009 by
Orion Books an imprint of the Orion Publishing Group Ltd
Orion House, 5 Upper St Martin's Lane, London WC2H 9EA
An Hachette Livre UK Company

A CIP catalogue record for this book is available from the British Library.

ISBN: 978 1 409 10469 8

Designed by www.carrstudios.co.uk
Printed in Spain by Grupo Cayfo, Impresia Ibérica,S.A.

The Orion Publishing Group's policy is to use papers that are natural,
renewable and recyclable and made from wood grown in sustainable
forests. The logging and manufacturing processes are expected to
conform to the environmental regulations of the country of origin.

Every effort has been made to fulfil requirements with regard to
reproducing copyright material. The author and publisher will be glad
to rectify any omissions at the earliest opportunity.

www.orionbooks.co.uk

PICTURE CREDITS

Getty: 2, 3, 4, 10, 13 (top), 16,
20 (left), 23 (top), 24, 27, 32,
43, 50, 53
Rex: 6, 7, 9, 15, 17, 18, 19, 20
(right), 21, 22, 23 (bottom), 25,
26 (top), 29, 30, 31, 33, 34,
35, 36, 38, 39, 40, 41, 42, 44,
45, 46 (top), 47, 48 (top), 51,
52, 54, 55, 56, 57, 60, 61
PA Photos: 5, 11, 12, 13 (bottom),
14, 28, 46 (bottom), 48 (bottom)
Big Pictures: 8, 26 (bottom), 37,
49, 59 (bottom)
Corbis: 58, 59 (top)

ACKNOWLEDGEMENTS

Molly Mitchell would like to
thank Neil Simpson, Amanda
Harris, Daniel Bunyard, Helen
Ewing, Rich Carr, Jane Sturrock
and Fiona McIntosh.